DELICIOUS FOOD
ON A BUDGET

DELICIOUS FOOD ON A BUDGET

RECIPE BOOK

ANGELA ORANYE

To order this book, contact Iconic Concepts Limited by phone on 07825313771, 07848920022 and 01279412418 or by email: *fuju78@ yahoo.com* or angelaoranye@yahoo.co.uk.

This book was printed in the United States of America.

Rev. date: 11/12/2013

To order additional copies of this book, contact:
Xlibris LLC
0-800-056-3182
www.xlibrispublishing.co.uk
Orders@xlibrispublishing.co.uk
307748

CONTENTS

BREAD PUDDING

INGREDIENTS

1] Brown bread
2] 6 eggs
3] 6 table spoons of sugar
4] 1cup of milk
5] Grinded bread crumbs
6] Cinnamon spice

HOW TO PREPARE IT

1] Get a mixing bowl; beat the 6 eggs inside it and the sugar.
2] Add the grinded bread crumbs and mix well with a wooden spoon, add the cup of milk and mix well until you have a smooth constituency.
3] Get a baking tin and put the mixture in it, bake at 140 degrees for 30mins.
4] When it is ready take it out of the oven and cut into slices.
5] Serve a slice with custard.

BAKED BEANS AND TUNA SAUCE

INGREDIENTS

1] 4 Tins of baked beans
2] 2 cans of tuna
3] Half tomato puree
4] Spices of your choice
5] Vegetable/olive oil
6] Chicken stock

HOW TO PREPARE IT

1] Get the 4tins of bake beans and rinse it under the tap, getting rid of all the sauce and put it on a plate.
2] Drain the tuna and put on a plate.
3] Get a sauce pan and put some oil in it.
6] Slice 1 onion and 3gloves of garlic and put in the sauce pan.
7] Mix the half tomato puree with water and put in a bowl, pour it in the sauce
8] Add the spices and chicken stock and allow to boil for a few minutes.
9] Add the baked beans and tuna to the sauce.
10] Serve with boiled potato.

COCONUT SAUCE WITH RICE

INGREDIENTS

1] 4 tins of coconut milk
2] 1 packet of chicken breast pieces
3] 1 packet of mixed vegetable
4] Vegetable oil
5] Chicken stock
6] Spices
7] 2 tablespoon of black or white pepper
8] 2 tablespoon of plain flour

HOW TO PREPARE IT

1] Heat up the sauce pan and add 2 spoons of vegetable oil.
2] Add the chicken breast pieces [cooked]
3] Open the 4 tins of coconut milk and add to the sauce pan.
4] Add the spices and black or white pepper to the sauce and mixed vegetable.
5] After the spices and mixed vegetable add the chicken stock and 2 tablespoon of plain flour and serve with boiled rice.

MASHY PEAS, BAKED BEANS AND TUNA SAUCE

INGREDIENTS

1] 1 packet of marshy peas
2] 4 tins of baked beans
3] 2 cans of tuna
4] Half a tube of tomato puree
5] Spices and vegetable oil
6] Chicken stock and salt

HOW TO PREPARE IT

1] Rinse the 4 tins of baked beans and put in a plate
2] Get a sauce pan and pour 2 cooking spoon of vegetable oil in the sauce pan
3] Add 1 big sliced onion and 4 gloves of sliced garlic
4] Then add half a tube of tomato puree and chicken stock
5] Add spices and salt to taste.
6] Let it boil for another few minutes and served with boiled potato or boiled rice

5

POTATO AND TUNA CAKES

INGREDIENTS

1] 1 packet of potato
2] 2 tins of tuna
3] 1pack of cheese spread
4] 1 teaspoon of salt

HOW TO PREPARE IT

1] Boil the potato in a sauce pan or pot and add salt.
2] When ready mash the potato in a bowl.
3] Mix the potato with 150g of cheese spread
4] Add the 2 cans of tuna and salt to taste
5] Mould into burger Shapes and put in a baking tray and bake at 160 degrees for 20 minutes
6] Serve with your favourite vegetable.

COUS COUS STIR FRY

INGREDIENTS

1] 1 packet of couscous 500g
2] Mixed vegetable
3] Garlic
4] Spices
5] Chicken stock
6] Onions
7] Sesame oil
8] One teaspoon of salt

HOW TO PREPARE IT

1] Get wok, put sesame oil in it.
2] Slice the onions and garlic and put in the wok
3] Put the mixed vegetable to fry
4] Soak the couscous in hot boiling water for 5 minutes
5] When the couscous is ready add it to the wok
6] Mix well and serve a portion to eat

POTATO AND CHICKEN SAUCE

INGREDIENTS

1] One packet of potato
2] One packet of chicken breast pieces
3] Half a tube of tomato puree
4] Chicken stock
5] Spices
6] Vegetable oil
7] 1 teaspoon of salt

HOW TO PREPARE IT

1] Cut the potato into tiny pieces
2] Get a sauce pan and pour 2 serving spoons of vegetable oil
3] Cut 1 big onions and put in it
4] Add the tomato puree and stir
5] Add the spices and the cooked potato pieces
6] Mix well and add the salt.

RICE NOODLES & CHICKEN STIR FRY

INGREDIENTS

1] One packet of rice noodles
2] One packet of chicken breast pieces
3] Chinese vegetable of your choice
4] Sesame oil
5] Salt and black pepper

HOW TO PREPARE IT

1] Soak your rice noodles in a bowl of boiling water.
2] Get your wok ready and put some sesame oil in it.
3] Put your Chinese vegetable next
4] Add your cooked chicken breast pieces
5] Salt and pepper to taste.
6] Add the rice noodles and mix well
7] Leave to shimmer for 5 minutes.
8] Serve on a plate and enjoy.

9

SPINACH, SPRING GREEN AND GREEN VEGETABLE STEW

INGREDIENTS

1] Spinach, spring green, and green vegetable
2] Meat of your choice
3] Two cooking spoons of vegetable oil
4] Half a tube of tomato puree
5] Meat stock
6] Salt and pepper
7] Maggi cube

HOW TO PREPARE IT

1] Get a pot; pour some vegetable oil in it
2] Slice one big onion in it
3] Put the half a tube of tomato puree in the sauce pan and add the meat stock
4] Let it boil for a while
5] Add the Maggi cube, salt and pepper.
6] Add the washed vegetables to the pot.
6] Leave to boil for another 2 minutes.

CHICKEN BREAST PIECES AND SWEET CORN WRAP

INGREDIENTS

1] Chicken breast pieces
2] Sweet corn
3] 'Tortilla' wrap [wholemeal or white]
4] Sauce of choice [mayonnaise and ketchup]

HOW TO PREPARE IT

1] Get a plate and a wrap from the pack
2] Spread it out on the plate
3] Put your choice of sauce
4] Chicken breast pieces and sweet corn
5] Wrap it and enjoy.

FISHERMAN'S PIE

INGREDIENTS

1] A bag of potato
2] Salmon, cod fillet and mackerel fish
3] Cheese spread and salt

HOW TO PREPARE IT

1] Boil the potato in a sauce pan
2] Put a pot on the fire and add two cooking spoons of vegetable oil
3] Slice one big onion and put in it
4] Put the cheese spread and salt in it
5] Put the salmon, cod fillet and mackerel fillet the sauce pan
6] Mash the potato in a bowl with butter and milk
7] Put the sauce in a casserole dish and put the mash potato on it. Put in the oven at 160 degrees for 20mins.
8] Serve after 20mins and enjoy.

SHEPHERD'S PIE

INGREDIENTS

1] A leg of beef
2] potato
3] Vegetable oil and spices of your choice
4] Salt & black or white pepper

HOW TO PREPARE

1] Boil the leg of beef
2] Boil the bag of potato
3] Get a sauce pan and put vegetable oil in it. Make sure the beef is very soft falling of the bone and mash it.
4] In the sauce pan add the mashed meat and the spices
5] Add pepper and salt to taste
6] Get a casserole dish and put the sauce inside it Add the mashed potato on it.
7] Put the casserole dish in a preheated oven at 160 degrees for 20 minutes
8] After 20 minutes serve a portion and enjoy it.

NEW POTATOES, PARSNIP AND BUTTERNUT SQUASH SAUCE

INGREDIENTS

1] New potatoes, parsnip, butternut squash and Mixed Vegetable
2] Mixed vegetable
3] Two cooking spoon of cooking oil
4] Cheese spread
5] Spices
6] Salt and pepper
7] Half a cup of water
8] Chicken stock

HOW TO PREPARE

1] Boil the potatoes, parsnip and butternut squash.
2] Get a sauce pan and add the two cooking spoon of vegetable oil
3] Slice one big onion and three gloves of garlic.
4] Add the mixed vegetable
5] Mix the cheese spread with water and add it.
6] Add the spices, salt and pepper
7] Add the water and chicken stock
8] Add the potatoes, parsnip and butternut squash and mix well.

SPECIAL MIXED SALAD

INGREDIENTS

Lettuce, carrots, cooked shrimps,
sweet corn, fresh apple, raisin, beetroot,
Tuna in brine, frankfurters (smoked with natural beechwood) and mayonnaise

HOW TO PREPARE IT

1] Empty all the canned food in a plate and rinse it.
2] Cut the sausage and beetroot into tiny
But sizeable chunks and put in a bowl
3] Mix all together putting it layer by layer.
4] Mix with mayonnaise when you serve a portion

COUSCOUS FRIED
VEGETABLE WITH SHRIMPS

INGREDIENTS

One packet of COUSCOUS 500g, garlic
mixed vegetable, mixed peppers, one big onions, shrimps, spices of
your choice, two cooking spoons of vegetable oil, sesame oil

HOW TO PREPARE IT

1] Get a sauce pan and put the two cooking spoons of vegetable
   oil
2] Slice the onions and garlic and put in it.
3] Put the packet of shrimps
4] Add one cooking spoon of sesame oil
5] Add the mixed vegetable and mixed peppers
6] Add the spices and the couscous in a bowl of boing water to
   soak and be ready.
7] Add the spices and the couscous and mix well.

16

SWEETPOTATO, BUTTERNUT SQUASH, PARSNIP AND GARLIC BAKE

INGREDIENTS

1] One packet of Sweet potato
2] One packet of parsnip
3] One packet of butternut squash
4] Garlic
5] 250ml of cream
6] Salt & Pepper
7] Olive oil and Chicken breast pieces

HOW TO PREPARE IT

Peel and cut the boiled sweet potato, parsnip and butternut squash into wedges. wash a baking tray and put the root vegetables inside in layers and chicken breast pieces pouring a bit of cream over it in layers. Bake in a preheated oven at 140 degrees until the root vegetables are cooked and ready to eat and the top layer golden brown.

CHICKEN BREAST PIECES AND SAUSAGE WITH PITTA BREAD

INGREDIENTS

1] One packet of pitta bread
2] One packet of chicken breast pieces.
3] One packet of sausages
4] Your favourite sauce
5] One tin of sweet corn
6] Lettuce one pack
7] Three ripe tomatoes

HOW TO PREPARE IT

1] Get your pitta bread [brown or white]
2] Toast it in the toaster
3] When ready open one side of the pitta bread and add your cooked chicken breast pieces and one sausage cut into pieces and put inside the pitta bread.
4] Add the lettuce one ripe tomato sliced and two tablespoon of sweet corn.
5] Add your favourite sauce and enjoy.

PASTA TUNA AND
SWEETCORN SALAD

INGREDIENTS

1]   One packet of [brown or white pasta]
2]   One tin of sweetcorn
3]   One tin of tuna
4]   Four tablespoons of mayonnaise

HOW TO PREPARE IT

1]   Boil the pasta [white or brown] in a saucepan.
2]   When ready drain the water from the pasta
3]   Add the tuna and sweetcorn and mix well.
4]   Add the four tablespoons of mayonnaise and mix well
5]   Put in a bowl and in the fridge.
6]   Serve a portion from the fridge and enjoy.

19

BAKED BEANS AND TUNA

INGREDIENTS

1]   4 Tins of baked beans
2]   2 cans of tuna
3]   1 big onions
4]   3 gloves of garlic
5]   2 cooking spoons of vegetable oil or your preferred oil
6]   Half a tube of tomato puree
7]   Spices [your preferred spices]
8]   Chicken stock or preferred stock
9]   Salt
10]   Pepper

HOW TO PREPARE IT

1]   Rinse the four tins of baked beans under the tap for all the juice to go out using a sieve and put on a plate.
2]   Drain the water or oil in the tuna and put on a plate.
3]   Get a saucepan and put the two cooking spoons of cooking oil in it.
4]   Slice the onions and garlic and put in the oil, let it fry until golden brown.
5]   Put the half tube of tomato puree in a bowl and mix with water and pour everything in the saucepan.
6]   Let it shimmer for 5mins and add your preferred spice.
7]   Add your preferred stock or chicken stock and let it shimmer for a few minutes.
8]   Add salt and pepper to it.
9]   Finally add all the baked beans and all the tuna and mix well.

20

SPAGETTI CHICKEN MEAT BALLS AND MUSHROOMS IN WHITE SAUCE

INGREDIENTS

1] 1 packet of mushrooms
2] 1 packet of spaghetti [white or brown]
3] 500g of chicken breast
4] Cheese spread
5] Spices
6] Salt
7] Pepper
8] 4 Gloves of garlic
9] Vegetable oil or preferred oil

HOW TO PREPARE IT

1] Boil the spaghetti in a pot with a teaspoon of salt.
2] When cooked drain the water and put in a bowl.
3] Get a saucepan and put 2 cooking spoons of your preferred cooking oil in it.
4] Slice one big onions and 4 gloves of garlic and put inside the saucepan
5] Slice the mushroom and wash it, putting it inside the saucepan
6] Add the cheese spread and spices and leave to boil for 5mInutes.
7] Add your Preferred stock and leave to boil for a Few minute
8] Add the cooked chicken breast to the saucepan and leave to boil for a few minute.
9] After a few minute serve a portion of the spaghetti on a plate with the chicken white sauce and mushroom and enjoy.

21

PASTA SHRIMPS AND OLIVES BAKE

INGREDIENTS

1]   One packet of pasta 500g [white or brown]
2]   One packet of shrimps
3]   Mixed peppers
4]   2 cooking spoons of vegetable oil or preferred oil.
5]   Spices
6]   4 gloves of garlic
7]   Your preferred stock
8]   Salt
9]   Pepper
10] Preferred cheese
11] One tin of black olives or preferred choice.

HOW TO PREPARE IT

1]   Boil your preferred pasta [brown or white] in a pot with water and add one teaspoon of salt.
2]   leave it to cook, when the pasta is cooked drain it and put it in a bowl.
3]   Get a saucepan put your 2 cooking spoons of vegetable oil or preferred oil.
4]   Slice one big onions and 4 gloves of garlic and put inside the saucepan.
5]   Dice the 3 mixed peppers and add to it
6]   Put all the shrimps inside and leave to shimmer for 5 minutes.
7]   Add your preferred stock and let it boil for a few minute.
8]   Add your spices, salt and pepper and let it boil for 2 minutes

9] Get a baking dish and put the sauce inside it and the cooked pasta on it.

10] Sprinkle cheese on it your preferred cheese and put in the oven for 20 mins at 160 degrees.

11] Open your tin of preferred olives and sprinkle on it.

12] Serve a portion on a plate and enjoy.

VEGETABLE AND CHICKEN BAKE

INGREDIENTS

1] Your favourite vegetable
2] Chicken breast pieces
3] Cheese spread
4] Your favourite cooking oil
5] Salt
6] Pepper

HOW TO PREPARE IT

1] Get a bowl, put your favourite vegetable inside it.
2] Put your cooked chicken breast inside it and mix well
3] Put the 500g of cheese spread and mix well
4] Add two cooking spoons of olive oil
5] Salt and pepper to taste
6] Put everything in a baking dish and bake in the oven at 160 Degrees for 15minutes.

23

SPAGETTI IN TOMATO SAUCE WITH SALT AND PEPPER CHICKEN

INGREDIENTS

1] One packet of spaghetti [brown or white]
2] 1 packet of chicken breast
3] Half a tube of tomato puree
4] Your favourite spices
5] Two cooking spoons of olive oil
6] Chicken stock one cup
7] Salt
8] Pepper
9] 1 cup of flour

HOW TO PREPARE IT

1] Boil the spaghetti in a pot of fresh water from the tap.
2] Get your saucepan and put your favourite cooking oil in it [two cooking spoons]
3] Slice one big onion and 4 gloves of garlic
4] Put half the tube of tomato puree inside
5] Chicken stock one cup and your favourite spices
6] Salt and pepper to taste
7] Add all the spaghetti and mix well
8] Get a bowl put all the chicken breast inside it [cooked chicken breast]
9] Add one teaspoon each of salt and pepper
10] Add the one cup of flour and mix well

11] Get your frying pan and put cooking oil in it and fry the chicken breast until golden brown.

12] You put some spaghetti on a plate and some chicken breast and enjoy.

COUSCOUS IN TOMATO SAUCE AND MIXED VEGETABLE WITH SALT AND PEPPER SEAFOOD

INGREDIENTS

1] Any seafood of your choice [a packet]
2] One packet of COUSCOUS 500g
3] Half a tube of tomato puree
4] 2 cooking spoons of your favourite cooking oil.
5] Your favourite spices
6] One packet of mixed vegetable
7] Salt and pepper
8] Half a cup of water

HOW TO PREPARE IT

1] Soak your couscous in a bowl of hot water
2] Get your saucepan and put two cooking spoons of your favourite cooking oil in it.
3] Slice one big onions and put in it.
4] Add your favourite spice
5] Mix the half tube of tomato puree with water and put inside the saucepan
6] Add your mixed vegetable and half a cup of water
7] Add salt and pepper and leave to boil for a few minutes.
8] Put the couscous in the sauce pan and mix thoroughly
9] Serve a portion and enjoy.

CHICKEN AND BACON IN COCONUT SAUCE AND VEGETABLE RICE

INGREDIENTS

1] 8 Pieces of chicken breast
2] 1 packet of unsaltedbacon
3] 4 tins of coconut milk
4] Brown rice or basmatic rice 500g
5] 1 packet of mixed vegetable
6] Salt
7] Pepper
8] 1 big onions
9] Four gloves of garlic
10] Two cooking spoons of cooking oil of your preferred cooking oil

HOW TO PREPARE IT

1] Wash 6 parts of chicken breast and put in a pot, slice half the onions and put in it and 2 gloves of garlic and boil
2] When the chicken breast is ready put on a plate and leave on the side.
3] Put the oven on at 160degrees, take the chicken breast on the plate, taking one after the other wrap each bacon on the chicken breast and put in the oven to bake for 10mins
4] Get your sauce pan and put the two cooking spoons of your preferred cooking oil in it
5] Slice half of the onions and the two remaining gloves of garlic and put in the saucepan

6]   Open the 4 tins of coconut milk and add in it, leave it to boil for a few minutes.
7]   Add the chicken and bacon wrap to the coconut sauce
8]   Add the mixed vegetable and salt and pepper and mix thoroughly
9]   Add your brown rice or basmatic rice 500g and mix well.
10] Serve a portion of the vegetable rice in coconut sauce and the chicken and bacon wrap and enjoy.

PASTA AND SPINACH WITH SALT AND PEPPERED CHICKEN

INGREDIENTS

1] Pasta white or brown
2] 1 packet of fresh spinach
3] Blue cheese or favourite cheese
4] Two cooking spoons of cooking oil your preferred choice
5] Spices and herbs
6] 1 packet of chicken breast
7] Pepper
8] Salt

HOW TO PREPARE IT

1] Boil the pasta in a pot [brown or white]
2] Slice your spinach and put on a plate
3] Get your saucepan and put your two cooking spoons of cooking oil inside it
4] Slice one big onions and put inside it
5] Slice three gloves of garlic and put in it
6] Put spinach, spices, and herb inside it and let it boil for a while
7] Salt and pepper to taste
8] Add your blue cheese or preferred cheese and let it shimmer for 5mins mix thoroughly
9] Add your boiled pasta to the sauce pan and mix EN thoroughly
10] Put your deep fryer on setting it at 180degrees for frying poultry products
11] Put your cooked chicken breast in a bowl and add salt and pepper to it one teaspoon each, mix thoroughly.

12] Put your cooked chicken breast in the deep fat fryer and fry it until golden brown; then remove it and put on a paper towel to drain any excess oil

13] Serve a portion of the pasta in a plate and salt and pepper chicken and enjoy.

27

PIZZA [CHICKEN, VEGETABLE AND MUSHROOM]

INGREDIENTS

1] Get your pizza bread [brown or white]
2] 1 packet of chicken breast cooked and diced
3] Mushrooms and mixed peppers or your favourite vegetable
4] 4 tablespoons of tomato puree
5] One cup of cheese

HOW TO PREPARE IT

1] Take your pizza bread and rub the 4 tablespoons of tomato puree on it
2] Get your sauce pan and put two cooking spoons of your preferred cooking oil
3] Slice one big onion and put in it
4] Slice two gloves of garlic and put in it
5] Add the sliced mushrooms and chopped mixed peppers leave it to shimmer for 5minutes
6] Add the cooked chicken breast and mix well.
7] Put everything on your pizza bread
8] Sprinkle the one cup of cheese on the pizza bread and put in the oven at 140degrees for 20minutes or as desired.
9] After 20 minutes serve a portion on a plate and enjoy.

CHICKEN BURGER

INGREDIENTS

1] 6 parts of chicken breast
2] White or brown buns
3] Cheese spread
4] Lettuce one medium one
5] 4 big and ripe tomatoes
6] Salt
7] Pepper

HOW TO PREPARE IT

1] Put the 6 parts of chicken breast in a pot
2] Slice one big onion and put in it
3] Slice two gloves of garlic and put in it
4] Salt and pepper
5] When the chicken breast is cooked put in a bowl and put the cheese spread in it and mash it with a fork the cheese spread will help to bind it together
Mould it into burger shapes and put in the baking tray
6] Put the oven on 160degrees and bake for 20minutes.
7] Take one bun cut it in middle, butter it and put one chicken burger in it.
8] Cut the tomatoes and lettuce and put inside the bun
9] Put your favourite sauce inside and enjoy.

SAUSAGE WRAP

INGREDIENTS

1] White or brown tortilla wraps
2] One packet of frankfurters
3] Mayonnaise
4] Ketchup
5] One medium lettuce
6] 4 large tomatoes

HOW TO PREPARE IT

1] Get your tortilla wrap brown or white
2] Put one teaspoon of mayonnaise on the wrap spread it around the wrap.
3] Put one sausage in each wrap
4] Put the sliced lettuce and tomato
5] Put the ketchup or your favourite sauce and wrap it enjoy it hot or cold.

BOILED POTATO CARROTS AND MACKERL FISH

INGREDIENTS

1] A packet of new potato or your favourite potato 500g
2] One big mackerel fish
3] One cheese spread 500g
4] Your favourite herb
5] Salt
6] Pepper

HOW TO PREPARE IT

1] Get your pot and put your potato in it [using new potato boil it with the skin on]
2] Get your bowl and put the fish inside it, put three table spoons of cheese spread inside it and mix well
3] Put your favourite herb and mix well
4] Put one teaspoon each of salt and pepper and mix well
5] Put on the grill until both sides are brown
6] Put the sliced carrots on plate and in the microwave for 5minutes
7] Serve a portion of the potato with carrots and mackerel and enjoy.

31

FRIED RICE WITH SALT AND PEPPERED CHICKEN

INGREDIENTS

1] Brown rice or basmati rice 500g
2] A packet of mixed vegetable
3] Two cooking spoons of vegetable oil
4] One packet of chicken breast pieces
5] Your preferred spice
6] One big onion
7] 4 gloves of fresh garlic
8] A packet of shrimps 500g
9] Two cooking spoons of sesame oil
10] Salt
11] Pepper black or white

HOW TO PREPARE IT

1] Boil the rice in a pot all of it
2] Get your saucepan and put the two cooking spoons of vegetable oil and the two cooking spoons of sesame oil inside the saucepan
3] Slice one big onion and 4 gloves of garlic
4] Add your packet of shrimps
5] Add salt and pepper and let the sauce shimmer for 5 minutes
6] Add the boiled rice and mix well
7] Put the deep fat fryer on 180degrees for frying meat let the oil be hot
8] Put the cooked chicken breast pieces in a bowl.

9] Add one teaspoon each of salt and pepper to the chicken in the bowl and mix well.

10] Put the chicken breast in the deep fat fryer until golden brown remove and put on a paper towel to drain oil.

11] Serve a portion and enjoy.

VEGETABLES AND TUNA BAKE

INGREDIENTS

1] Your favourite vegetables
2] Four tablespoons of cheese spread
3] Your favourite cooking oil [2cooking spoons of it]
4] 2 tins of tuna
5] Salt
5] Pepper
6] Two cooking spoons of sesame oil

HOW TO PREPARE IT

1] Get your saucepan and put two cooking spoons of your favourite oil in your saucepan and two cooking spoons of sesame oil
2] Slice one big onion and 3 gloves of garlic and put in it
3] Put your favourite vegetables in it and mix well
4] Add salt and pepper and let it boil for a few minutes
5] Add the two cans of tuna and mix well
6] Put in a dish and put in the oven at 160degrees for 10minutes.
11] Serve a portion and enjoy

33

BUTTER NUT SQUASH CHIPS AND ROAST CHICKEN

INGREDIENTS

1] 2 whole butternut squash
2] 8 parts of chicken
3] 4 tablespoon of cheese spread
4] Your favourite spice and herb
5] One tin of coconut milk
6] 2 cooking spoons of olive oil
7] Salt and pepper

HOW TO PREPARE IT

1] Peel your butternut nut squash and cut into wedges
2] Put the deep fryer on 160 degrees for frying, put the washed butternut squash into a bowl and add salt to it
3] Put in the deep fat fryer to fry until golden brown
4] Put on a paper towel to remove excess oil
5] Get your bowl and put your 8 parts of chicken inside, put your 4 spoons of cheese spread and mix well
5] Add your coconut milk and mix well
6] Add salt and pepper and mix well
7] Put all the contents in a baking tray and bake in the oven until golden brown at the top.
8] Serve a portion of the butternut squash chips and the roast chicken and enjoy.

34

CHICKEN SOUP WITH GARLIC ROAST POTATOES

INGREDIENTS

1] A bag of baking potatoes 500g
2] 8 parts of chicken breast
3] One whole Garlic
4] 2 cooking spoons of olive oil
5] Your favourite spice and herb
6] Salt
7] Pepper
8] One big onion

HOW TO PREPARE IT

1] Take the 8 parts of chicken breast and wash it and cut them in cubes and put in a cooking pot to boil.
2] Slice one big onion and put in it
3] Cut three gloves of garlic and put in it.
4] Add your favourite spice and herb
5] Add salt and pepper to it and let it boil until the chicken is cooked then it is ready.
6] Get your bag of potato peel it, wash it, and slice it thinly.
7] Get your baking tray and put your potatoes in layers putting garlic pieces in between and sprinkling 2 cooking spoons of olive oil on it
8] Put in the oven at 140 degrees until the potato is cooked
9] Serve a portion of the chicken soup and roast garlic potato and enjoy.

FISH VEGETABLE AND POTATO SOUP

INGREDIENTS

1] Your favourite fish
2] Your favourite vegetable
3] 4 gloves of garlic
4] 1 big onion
5] A pack of potato
6] Your favourite spice and herb
7] Salt
8] Pepper

HOW TO PREPARE IT

1] Get your potato peel it, wash it and dice it
2] Get your favourite vegetable wash it and put in a pot
3] Slice one big onion and four gloves of garlic and put inside the pot
4] Put your favourite spice and herb inside it
5] Wash and cut your favourite fish into cubes and put in the pot
6] Add one teaspoon each of salt and pepper and let it boil until the potato and fish is cooked
7] Serve a portion and enjoy.

PASTA WITH VEGETABLE AND SHRIMPS

INGREDIENTS

1] Brown or white pasta 500g
2] Your favourite vegetables
3] A pack of Shrimps [cooked and peeled] 500g
4] 2 cooking spoons of olive oil
5] 2 tablespoon of sesame oil
6] Your favourite spice and herb
7] 2 tablespoons of cheese spread
8] 1 big onion
9] 4 gloves of garlic
10] Half a cup of chicken stock

HOW TO PREPARE IT

1] Boil your pasta in a pot of water with one teaspoon of salt
2] Get your saucepan and put two cooking spoons of olive oil and two tablespoons of sesame oil in it
3] Put the shrimps inside and let it boil for 5 minutes
4] Add your favourite vegetable and two tablespoons of cheese spread
5] Add your chicken stock [half a cup] and let it boil for 5 minutes
6] Add your favourite spice and herb and mix well
7] Add your cooked pasta and mix well
8] Let it boil for 5 minutes and it is ready serve a portion and enjoy.

www.ingramcontent.com/pod-product-compliance
Lightning Source LLC
Chambersburg PA
CBHW050431290526
45786CB00003B/1484